HERO DOGS!

True Stories of Amazing Animal Heroes!

Mary Quattlebaum

NATIONAL GEOGRAPHIC

WASHINGTON, D.C.

Since 1888, the National Geographic Society has
funded more than 12,000 research, exploration, and
preservation projects around the world. The Society
receives funds from National Geographic Partners,
LLC, funded in part by your purchase. A portion of
the proceeds from this book supports this vital work.
To learn more, visit natgeo.com/info.

NATIONAL GEOGRAPHIC and Yellow Border
Design are trademarks of the National Geographic
Society, used under license.

For more information, visit nationalgeographic.com,
call 1-800-647-5463, or write to the following address:

National Geographic Partners
1145 17th Street N.W.
Washington, D.C. 20036-4688 U.S.A.

Visit us online at nationalgeographic.com/books

For librarians and teachers: ngchildrensbooks.org

More for kids from National Geographic:
kids.nationalgeographic.com

For information about special discounts for bulk
purchases, please contact National Geographic Books
Special Sales: specialsales@natgeo.com

For rights or permissions inquiries, please contact
National Geographic Books Subsidiary Rights:
bookrights@natgeo.com

Art directed by Sanjida Rashid
Designed by Ruth Ann Thompson

National Geographic supports K–12
educators with ELA Common Core
Resources. Visit natgeoed.org/
commoncore for more information.

Trade paperback ISBN: 978-1-4263-2819-0
Reinforced library edition ISBN: 978-1-4263-2820-6

Printed in China
17/RRDS/1

Table of CONTENTS

Wilshire and firefighters of the Los Angeles Fire Department.

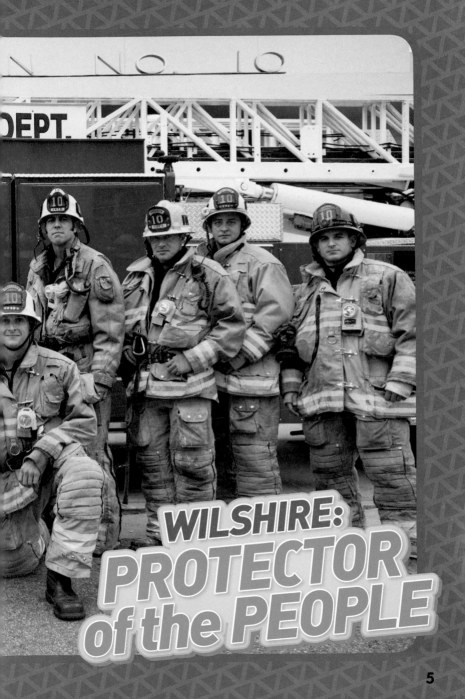

WILSHIRE: PROTECTOR of the PEOPLE

The mysterious pup

Chapter 1

PESKY PUP

Ryan Penrod looked down at the pup on the fire station's doorstep. It was six o'clock on a March morning. He was about to start his shift at Fire Station 29 in Los Angeles, California, U.S.A. Where had the pup come from?

The pup looked up at Ryan. At that moment, he seemed to decide that Ryan was his new best friend. "Woof," he said, wagging his tail.

The other firefighters filled Ryan in. The night before, a girl and her parents had come to the fire station on busy Wilshire (sounds like WILL-shur) Boulevard. She was crying because she had to give up her puppy. The owner of her apartment building said the puppy could no longer live there. He made too much noise! He barked and whined, and he disturbed the other people who lived in the building. The building's owner said the girl had to find the pup a new home immediately. Or she had to take him to the animal shelter. The firefighters wanted to help. They voted to let the pup stay.

So that's how the pup ended up at the fire station, and that's how he got his name: Wilshire.

Wilshire had a new name and a home, but no one knew what to do with him. He barked and jumped and ran around. "He was very excited and confused," said Ryan. Wilshire wasn't used to noises, like bells and sirens. He wasn't used to big fire trucks. And there were so many people! Sixteen firefighters, including Ryan, worked at the station at the same time.

Ryan began to take charge of the pup, which helped Wilshire to settle down. That night he slept in a dog bed beside Ryan's bed at the fire station. He waited for Ryan to feed him the next day. But then he began to get into trouble. He snuck food from the firefighters' table. He chewed on their boots. He slipped out the door and ran down the street.

Ryan knew Wilshire needed to be trained. The pup was four months old, and no one had taught him to "come" or "sit." No one had set boundaries. Wilshire was a breed of dog called a Dalmatian (sounds like dal-MAY-shun). They are smart dogs. Ryan hoped Wilshire would learn quickly.

He emailed a famous dog expert named Cesar Millan and asked for help. Cesar came to the fire station, and he taught Wilshire many important lessons. He also trained Ryan and the other firefighters to be more aware of Wilshire's needs.

Cesar said that only one person should be in charge of Wilshire, to avoid confusing the pup. Wilshire needed regular exercise. He needed to eat at regular times. He needed to learn to obey rules, like "do not sneak

Did You Know?

Dalmatians are white with many small spots that are either black or dark brown.

food" and "do not chew boots or equipment."

Wilshire learned from Cesar and so did Ryan. Cesar spoke in a firm, clear voice. He never yelled or lost his temper. He gave Wilshire treats for good behavior. He taught Wilshire rules to keep him safe and to help him to become a good member of the fire station team.

Ryan saw that Wilshire was becoming a relaxed, respectful dog. The pup was eager to work and obey. Maybe Wilshire could learn something else, something more complicated. Maybe Wilshire could learn how to help save lives.

There are many kinds of heroes, Ryan knew. Some heroes perform a single act of bravery. Perhaps they pull a drowning child from a lake or rescue an adult from a burning building. Others become heroes after a long period of time, like Martin Luther King, Jr., the great civil rights leader, or Florence Nightingale, a nurse. She tended to many sick and wounded people, and she started a school to train other nurses. Through their words and actions, heroes like King and Nightingale help to make the world a better, safer place.

Ryan talked about his idea with Cesar. Cesar asked Clint Rowe to help. Clint has trained animals for movies and TV shows. He has trained many dogs. He even trained a bear once! Maybe Clint could help a spunky Dalmatian pup. Maybe he could teach Wilshire how to be a fire safety hero.

At the time, Cesar had a TV show about dog training and behavior. It was called *Dog Whisperer*. He asked Clint, Ryan, and Wilshire to be part of his show. Millions of people watched as Clint taught Wilshire and Ryan to work as a team.

Wilshire learned to act out many important fire safety tips. People loved watching the intelligent pup, but they were also learning something very important. They were learning what to do in case of a fire emergency. They were also learning how to prevent fires in the first place. Wilshire was only a puppy, but he was on his way to becoming a hero.

Black, White, and Red: A Dalmatian History

In the late 1600s, Dalmatians were popular "coach dogs." When their owners traveled, the dogs trotted beside the carriages. They helped to soothe the horses and be on the lookout for robbers. Dalmatians were also used by firefighters in cities. They were like sirens! A Dalmatian would run ahead of the horse-drawn fire engine, barking.

The engine's red color and the dog's loud barking were a warning: *Out of the way! Fire ahead!* As the firefighters dealt with the blaze, the dog would stay close to calm the horses. Today's fire trucks don't have horses, but many are still red. And sometimes, a Dalmatian rides proudly inside, often headed to a safety presentation rather than an actual fire.

Wilshire shows kids how to stop, drop, and roll in case of a fire.

Chapter 2

SAVING LIVES

It was a sunny day at a park in Los Angeles. Children clapped as they watched Wilshire. Adults talked and smiled. There were many distractions. But Wilshire stayed focused on his important work. He and Ryan were doing their special show on fire and life safety. Ryan put some props on the stage, and Wilshire was ready. He knew what to do with each one.

Wilshire obeyed each of Ryan's verbal commands. Wilshire activated a smoke alarm. He crawled under a wooden model of a fire to show the crowd how to "get low and go" in case of a fire. He pressed the buttons on a phone with his nose to show how to dial 911. That is an important phone number to remember for any emergency.

People were amazed at Wilshire's next trick. They watched as the spotted dog suddenly stopped moving and stood very still. He then dropped to the ground, stretched out, and rolled. He was showing the crowd what to do if their clothes caught on fire. *Stop, drop, and roll!*

Everyone clapped. After the show, the children got into a long line. They wanted to pat Wilshire and take a photo with him. They wanted to look closely at his silver firefighter badge. Wilshire wanted to meet them, too. He wagged his tail as he greeted each child.

Ryan knows that Wilshire is a good teacher. He helps kids remember important safety tips. It's easy to forget when you read something, but when a dog shows you each tip, it stays in your mind.

"Wilshire's presentation is fun," said Ryan. "Kids love watching and learning from him."

Wilshire often helps Ryan teach health and fitness, too. If people eat unhealthy foods and don't get enough exercise, they

Did You Know?

The National Fire Protection Association uses a cartoon Dalmatian named Sparky to help people learn about fire safety.

may become overweight. Then they may suffer from health problems. Wilshire eats some fruits and vegetables to show how to make healthy food choices. He lifts a pretend barbell, or weight, to show the importance of working out. Ryan tells people that Wilshire runs on a treadmill at the fire station for 20 to 30 minutes a day. He exercises every morning with his firefighter friends. Go, Wilshire!

Although Wilshire usually doesn't help to fight the fires, he likes to travel in the fire truck, says Ryan. "What dog wouldn't love a ride with lights flashing and sirens blaring and the wind in his face?"

Once, Wilshire and Ryan were coming back from giving a talk at a school. Suddenly, their truck got a call. There was a fire! The firefighters quickly put on their gear as the truck raced to the scene.

"When we arrived," said Ryan, "we saw smoke coming from the building." They jumped off the fire truck, grabbing ladders, tools, and the hoses needed to put the fire out.

Wilshire stayed in the truck with the windows rolled up. "He was barking like crazy," said Ryan. He wanted to help!

Ryan and the other firefighters put out a fire on a stove in one of the apartments. No one was hurt. The smoke alarms had warned everyone to leave the building.

Wilshire's Tips for Fire Safety

• Make a plan with your family. Figure out a good escape route in case of a fire. Pick a safe meeting place outside so that the whole family can meet there. Make sure that pets have a way out, too.

• Practice your plan. Have fire drills twice a year.

- Check smoke alarms every month to make sure they work.

- In case of a fire, "get low and go." To avoid breathing smoke, crawl on your stomach so that you are close to the floor where the air is cool and clean.

- Know how to call emergency services.

- Never run if your clothes catch fire. That causes the fire to grow. Instead, remember: *Stop, drop, and roll.* Stop and cover your face with your hands; drop to the ground; lie flat and roll. This helps to put the fire out.

- Place a pet-alert sticker in your window. List the type and number of pets in your home. This helps rescue workers find and rescue your pets in an emergency.

The family with the fire was okay, but the children were scared. Their apartment was still filled with smoke. While it cleared, they waited outside. This was Wilshire's chance to help. Ryan brought the friendly dog over to visit. Wilshire helped the children feel calmer.

"They seemed to quickly forget about their fear," said Ryan. "They laughed a little when Wilshire wagged his tail and licked their faces."

To help people learn about fire safety, Wilshire and Ryan have traveled throughout Los Angeles and to other parts of the United States. They have visited schools and a children's hospital. They performed for the patients there.

Wilshire has also been on the news. Wilshire has even performed in local plays as a guest star. He played the dog characters in *Annie* and *Peter Pan and Tinker Bell—A Pirates Christmas*.

Wherever he goes, Wilshire shares his fire safety tips. Wilshire is also a good reminder. He shows that adopting a dog can help give that pooch a second chance. Millions of people have seen and learned from Wilshire.

Everyone should know about fire safety because this knowledge can save people's lives.

Wilshire at the fire station, wearing his badge

Chapter 3

DOG on the GO!

At the fire station, the day begins early for Wilshire and the other firefighters. He is fed every morning at 5:45. He helps to check the safety equipment to make sure everything is working. Firefighters must get ready quickly—within 60 seconds—when there is an emergency. They don't have time to look for or check their equipment at that point.

When they are working, firefighters also eat and sleep at the station. That way, they can respond to emergencies at any time of the day or night. To stay fit, Wilshire and the other firefighters run on treadmills every morning. The dog then watches as the firefighters do their chores, including cleaning the kitchen and dorm area.

They also train every day. Just like professional athletes, firefighters must practice their skills. They practice how to put out, or extinguish, different types of fires. But they don't just fight fires.

They also help people who are hurt. For example, they rescue people who are trapped in cars after accidents.

During a regular 24-hour shift, firefighters often deal with about 26 different emergencies or problems from the public. They are always busy!

Even when they are not dealing with problems, the firefighters and Wilshire are busy cleaning equipment and polishing the trucks (also called "rigs"). They also take turns cooking dinner. Usually, the meal is served between 5 and 7 p.m. But if a call comes in, the cook must turn off the stove and finish cooking after the hungry firefighters return.

Wilshire doesn't usually try to sneak food anymore, but one time he couldn't resist. The whole crew had to leave to respond to a fire just at the moment dinner was served. They left behind a stack of steaks. Yum! Those steaks sure smelled good. When Ryan and the others returned, guess what they found? Fewer steaks and a dog with a very full stomach!

After dinner, everyone helps to clean the dishes and kitchen. Bedtime is usually between 9 and 10 p.m. Even asleep, though, the firefighters are prepared. At the first sound of an alarm, they will jump up and slide down the pole and get on the rigs and out the fire station door, says Ryan.

For his first five years, Wilshire worked

Did You Know?

George Washington had a Dalmatian coach dog named Madame Moose.

at Fire Station
29. But then he
and Ryan were
moved to Fire
Station 10. Now
he works at the
station only when Ryan
is there, and he goes home
with Ryan after a busy shift. This gives
Wilshire a break from all the noise and
stress of the station.

At Ryan's home, the dog can relax
with Ryan's family. He can play with
Ryan's sons, Carter and Kayden. He can
snuggle with his favorite toy. He also likes
to sleep in Ryan's bed. That way he can
wake Ryan up at 5:45 in the morning.
Breakfast time!

More Than a Fire Dog

Dalmatians often are mascots for fire stations and for organizations that deal with fire safety. But these smart dogs do

other jobs as well. They have lots of energy and enjoy working. What else can they do? Dalmatians might be service dogs, assisting people in wheelchairs. They might be guide dogs to those who are blind or deaf. As therapy dogs, they visit patients in hospitals and nursing homes. People often smile and feel better when they pat a friendly pooch. Dalmatians make good pets, but they can be stubborn. They need lots of exercise and patient training from an early age.

Wilshire's not a puppy anymore, but he still has a lot of energy. He loves to run. He loves to wrestle and play tug of war with Ryan, Carter, and Kayden. He even helps out at home. Once Carter had a loose tooth, and he wanted Wilshire to help pull it out. Ryan tied one end of a string to Carter's tooth and the other to the dog's collar. "Go, Wilshire," he commanded. Well, Wilshire ran so fast that the tooth shot right out, and they never found it in the grass. But that's okay! Carter still got a nice present from the tooth fairy, and Wilshire got a big thank-you from Carter.

After his day off, Wilshire is ready to return to the station with Ryan. He's a fire dog, after all. He comes back to work rested and alert. Who knows what the day will hold? It's sure to be full of sirens and emergency calls and chances to teach the public about fire safety.

Wilshire is a great partner and friend. Wilshire "loves to work," says Ryan. Whenever Ryan starts packing a fire engine with Wilshire's gear, the dog wags his tail and spins with excitement. Wilshire knows he is going on a ride to help the public in some way. "He is the people's protector," said Ryan. "He is their hero."

Did You Know?

In the United States, National Fire Pup Day is October 1. It celebrates the brave dogs that have saved their owners from fires or have assisted firefighters.

Landa Coldiron and her bloodhound, Glory, follow the trail of a lost dog.

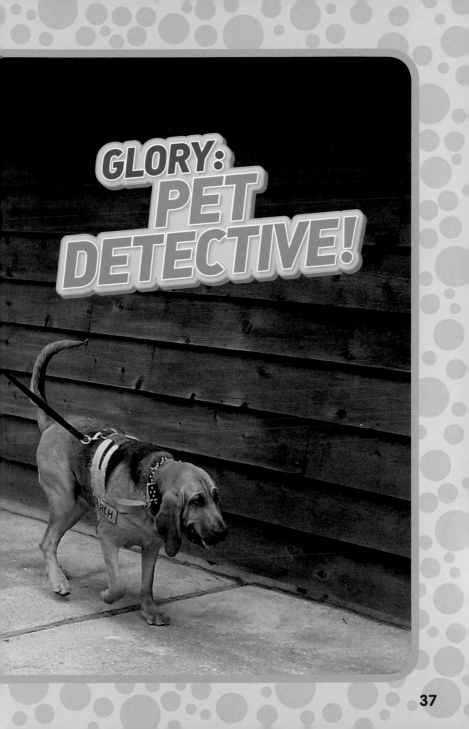

GLORY:
PET
DETECTIVE!

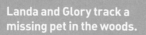

Landa and Glory track a missing pet in the woods.

Chapter 1

FINDING GOLDIE!

Glory sniffed the bedding. It belonged to a small dog named Goldie. Every living thing has a unique, or special, smell, and now Glory knew Goldie's.

"Search!" called Landa Coldiron, Glory's owner. The dog knew just what to do. She shook the rain off of her long ears, then she put her keen nose to the ground.

Glory was ready to use her strong sense of smell to follow, or trail, Goldie's scent.

Glory is a specially trained bloodhound. For nine years, she has worked for Landa's company, Lost Pet Detection. The company is near Sun Valley, California, U.S.A. Glory helps to find missing pets. On this day, she knew her job was to find Goldie.

Glory snuffled at the wet grass. First she sniffed to the right, then to the left. She sniffed at the air. Like any human or animal, little Goldie had left tiny traces of herself behind as she moved. These invisible bits of skin and fur were molecules called scent particles. These "Goldie particles" were in the air and on the grass, sidewalks, and other things that she had passed.

Did You Know?

The bloodhound is a type of hunting dog called a scent hound. They rely on their sense of smell to find and chase wild animals.

Now, the bloodhound was searching for that scent. Glory was trying to figure out which way the small dog had gone. Glory ignored other smells, even if they were stronger. She ignored the odors of people, other animals, and food. She focused only on Goldie's scent. This was important work!

Sniff, sniff went Glory's black nose. As she walked, she drew in Goldie's scent through her large nostrils. *Find Goldie.* Landa held Glory's long leash, called a long line, and followed her large black-and-tan dog. If anyone could find Goldie, it would be Glory. Bloodhounds can track scent better than any other breed of dog, and

Glory was a very hard-working bloodhound.

But there were big obstacles to finding Goldie. The little dog had run away from the pet sitter nine days ago. Her scent on grass and sidewalks had grown weaker with time. There was another problem: Goldie was a Pekingese (sounds like PEEK-uh-neez). That's a very small—or toy—breed of dog. Because she was small, Goldie was vulnerable (sounds like VUHL-ner-uh-buhl). She could have been picked up by a hawk or caught and eaten by coyotes. She had escaped in an area with freeways and traffic. Maybe a car had hit her.

Drip, drip, drip. The rain fell steadily, but it did not stop Glory. The bloodhound carefully "worked" the ground as she walked. This meant that Glory moved back and forth and searched for the scent rather than following it in a clear line. This is helpful when the scent is weak. Glory was trying to determine the general direction that Goldie had traveled.

Two other detection dogs, Diana and Rainbow, helped, too. They followed Glory and searched for anything that she may have missed, like Goldie's poop or her tawny fur.

Finally, Glory led Landa and the other dogs to a huge warehouse. Large, heavy machines clanked and rumbled as they moved crates from one spot outdoors to another. How could they find a tiny dog in this enormous, noisy place? But Glory had picked up the faint scent.

Then Glory and Landa ran into their biggest obstacle. They were not allowed to search the area without a special permit. They might have to wait for hours!

Landa was worried. She knew time was running out for Goldie. The little dog hadn't eaten for days. She might be hurt.

It took hours to get the permit. As they waited, Landa and the dogs searched for Goldie in other ways. Landa hung banners on her truck. The banners let people know about the search and whom to call with information on Goldie.

Finally, Landa heard some news about the permit from the warehouse manager. She could not get it until the next day. Because she and her dogs had driven many miles to the place where Goldie was lost, she knew they would have to spend the night in a hotel, far from home. Luckily, Landa had brought food for the dogs, just in case. After a long day in the rain, everyone needed to eat and rest.

The next morning, Landa and Glory returned to the warehouse. It was still raining, but Glory was eager to search. The bloodhound trotted past rows of crates. Goldie's scent grew stronger. Finally, Glory stopped at one crate and "alerted." This means that Glory held very still, which is her signal for "found." She looked at Landa and wagged her tail.

Hound History

Monks at the St. Hubert Monastery in a part of France that is now part of Belgium raised the first bloodhounds more than 1,300 years ago. The dogs were known as St. Hubert hounds. Every year, the monks gave several hounds as a gift to the king of France. Kings and noblemen valued their keen noses and courage. They were used to hunt large animals. In 1066, William the Conqueror and his soldiers left France and invaded England. They brought St. Hubert hounds with them. Over the centuries, bloodhounds have also been used to guard property and to track criminals.

And there was Goldie, huddled under some boards. She was weak from lack of food and water. Her fur was matted.

"Good dog, Glory!" Landa praised her hound. But Goldie was so frightened that she didn't realize Glory was a friend. She stared at the big dog and thought: *Danger!*

Goldie darted out from under the boards. She ran fast, fast, fast, trying to get away. She was so small and weak, though, that a warehouse worker caught her easily. He handed her gently to Landa. "You're safe now," Landa said, stroking Goldie.

Goldie's elderly owners were both very sick, so Landa phoned their daughter, Karin Wickam. Karin was so happy that she cried. And when Karin told her parents, they cried, too. What wonderful news!

Glory gets close
to pick up a scent.

Chapter 2

CAT RESCUE

oldie's story has a happy ending, thanks to Glory. In fact, Glory has given happy endings to the true tales of hundreds of missing pets.

Glory started her important search-and-rescue work when she was a pup. She was eight weeks old when Landa brought her to Lost Pet Detection. Landa started training her almost immediately.

Most dogs are naturally good at smelling. This is especially true of bloodhounds. A trainer helps them to learn what smell to focus on, how to follow it, and what to do when they find what they're looking for.

As a pup, Glory first learned how to find a dog or cat that was being held by a person. She got a big treat! That made her excited to learn more. Over time, Glory learned to follow a pet that had walked by 15 minutes earlier.

Next, Glory learned to follow a trail that was "aged." She was learning to follow scents that were increasingly older:

one day, two days, even one week old. Glory also learned to focus on the pet's unique scent and ignore any others.

"It takes a lot of dedication," said Landa. "You have to train every single day." But Glory enjoyed learning, and she really enjoyed the treats. Finally, when she was four years old, she was ready for a special test. If she passed, she would be a certified trailing dog.

The test was complicated. One part involved trailing, or following, a scent over different surfaces, including cement, dirt, and grass. The trail was almost a mile (1.6 km) long, with several turns and an intersection. Glory passed the test on the first try!

All the training helped to sharpen Glory's natural smelling instinct. She also learned to work as a team with the other dogs, like Diana and Rainbow, at Lost Pet Detection.

Although some bloodhounds are trained to search for humans, Glory and her doggy teammates focus only on lost pets. In addition to hundreds of dogs and cats, Glory has found two parrots and two tortoises. She also sniffed out a pet ferret trapped under a woodpile. These animals were lucky. They were found alive.

Often, lost pets are picked up by animal control officers, and their owners are able to find them, unharmed, at an animal shelter. That's why ID tags on collars and microchips are so important. The shelter staff then knows who to contact about the pet.

The Nose Knows

The inside of every dog's nose contains many scent receptors (sounds like ree-SEP-ters). These are tiny spots with nerves that connect to a certain part of the brain. When a dog smells something, this part of the brain helps to identify the odor and its age. Bloodhounds have more than 300 million scent receptors; most dogs have around 200 million. (Humans have only about 6 million.) No wonder the bloodhound can trail a scent better than any other breed!

Sometimes Glory finds only the remains of the pet. Unfortunately, many missing pets are killed by predators or by cars. In these cases, Glory might find the body or traces of blood, bits of fur or bones, or even fur in the predator's poop, or scat.

When this happens, Glory does not wag her tail. She only looks at Landa to signal that the lost animal has been found. This is sad, but at least the owners know what happened to their pet. They can stop searching and say goodbye.

Millions of dogs and cats go missing every year. Some pets run off while playing, others escape through open doors. Predators such as coyotes, foxes, hawks, and owls can be a big problem. They chase and frighten pets. Sometimes they catch and eat them.

A cat named Gladys lived in a part of California where coyotes often prowled. The black-and-white cat liked her freedom. She liked to go in and out of her cat door and explore the yard. But one day Gladys didn't return from her adventure. She didn't come home for dinner. Gladys's owner became very worried. She called and searched, but she did not see her cat. She did not hear her familiar *meow*.

Two days passed, then three and four. A week went by. Gladys had vanished.

The owner called Lost Pet Detection. Maybe Landa and Glory could help. The bloodhound sniffed Gladys's bedding and got right to work. Carefully, she traced the cat's unique scent across yards and sidewalks. She led Landa to a fence in front of a small tunnel. Then she stopped. *Gladys is close by,* she seemed to say. Landa peered inside the tunnel. It was partly covered, so it was hard to see anything. She listened. Nothing. She didn't smell cat urine, which has a very strong smell. It is usually the first clue that a cat is hiding nearby. There was no sign of Gladys. Glory and Landa waited and waited, hoping the cat would show up.

When it grew dark, Landa had to call Glory away. It was time to go home. She wondered whether Glory had made a mistake. Maybe Gladys had moved to a different place.

But then about a week later, the phone rang at Lost Pet Detection. It was Gladys's owner, with happy news. She said she had returned to the tunnel. She had wanted to check one more time. "Here, Gladys," the owner had called. She opened a can of cat food.

That's when the owner heard a very faint sound. *Meow. Meow.* It was Gladys! The cat was weak and hungry, but she was alive! She ran to her owner and snuggled.

Poor Gladys had been chased into the tunnel by a coyote, and she had been too frightened to leave, said Landa. Without Glory's help, the cat probably never would have been found.

Once again, Glory was a hero to a small, lost animal.

Glory and Landa pose for a picture during a ceremony to honor Glory's service.

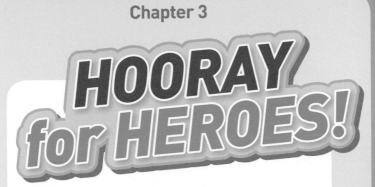

Chapter 3

HOORAY for HEROES!

Glory and Landa have been on many adventures together. They travel all around the state of California looking for lost pets.

"We've searched in water canals, deep in canyons, and along the ocean," said Landa. "We've searched on freeways, in cemeteries, and around a mansion." Wherever Glory goes, Landa follows.

Landa trusts Glory's keen nose. "She is amazing," said Landa. "When she is working, Glory is so focused that she doesn't hear me call her. I have to keep the long line on her or she would race off after the scent and leave me behind."

Once, they had to walk through mud so deep they could barely move. Glory's paws seemed to be coated in a heavy, gooey paste, but she kept slowly slogging forward. It was pretty funny.

"I couldn't stop laughing," said Landa.

But there is one place that Glory will not go: elevators. She decided one day that she did not like them. "Glory is a gentle giant, but she can be stubborn," said Landa. So, when they have to stay overnight on a search, Landa always makes sure to get a room on the first floor of a hotel. Otherwise, they would be walking up and down a lot of stairs!

Lost Pet Detection is very busy. The company focuses on pets in California. There are so many lost animals in California, they don't even have to leave the state. Glory usually goes on a search four to ten times a month.

The searches begin early. Landa and the dogs rise at four or five in the morning and drive to the place where the missing animal was last seen. A search might last from one to 12 hours, with occasional breaks. The search usually ends only when Glory and her doggy teammates find the lost pet or its remains.

Prevent Lost Pets

More than 10 million pets are lost or stolen each year, according to the American Humane Association.

To keep pets safe, owners should:

• Watch pets when outdoors. Predators can chase or pick them up and eat them.

- Make sure pets wear identifying (ID) tags or microchips.

- Close doors, windows, and gates.

- Be especially careful during holidays and parties. Pets might become excited and confused as people come and go. They can slip out an open door when their owners are busy.

When she isn't on a search, Glory stays at home with Landa and her husband and all their animals. In addition to two other search-and-rescue dogs, Glory pals around with horses, cats, and chickens.

On her days off, Glory likes to relax and sleep. She also continues to train, at least once a week. And she helps to train other dogs. Sometimes Landa will "ghost" a new dog after her. Landa explained that this means Glory will follow a scent and the other dog will follow Glory's scent as a way of learning to trail.

Glory always gets excited when she sees her search harness and long line.

She knows it's time to work, and she runs to Landa's truck. "Her favorite part of a search is the beginning," said Landa. Glory likes a new, fresh challenge.

In 2015, Glory received a special award from the American Humane Association. She had been voted the best search-and-rescue dog in the United States. How exciting! Glory now had a chance to win a big award—Hero Dog of the Year—at a ceremony in Beverly Hills, California. Seven other dogs were also competing. They had won for being excellent guide, military, or therapy dogs. There were many ways to be a hero!

On the evening of the big ceremony, Landa groomed Glory until her black-and-tan coat shone. Landa then changed into a long, beautiful gown. She was a little nervous, but Glory was very calm.

When they arrived, the giant stage blazed with light. People took Glory's photo. They petted her. "She loved the attention," said Landa.

Then the two took their place at an elegant table. A special friend greeted them: Karin! She was now living with Goldie, the Pekingese, in Idaho, U.S.A. Karin had traveled many miles to the Hero Dog ceremony. She wanted to cheer for Glory and to thank her again for finding Goldie. Karin will always be grateful to the friendly bloodhound.

Glory sniffed the air. *This is exciting, but not as exciting as the search for a lost pet,* Glory seemed to say. As the ceremony began, Glory lay down at Landa's feet. She snuffled gently and took a little nap.

Although Glory didn't win the top prize, she received a lovely glass statue for her excellent work as a search-and-rescue dog.

"I was so grateful to be honored for the work we do," said Landa.

Glory is a hero, but she likes the work better than a fancy award. The bloodhound never naps when she is on a search. Two days after the ceremony, Glory was back at work, trailing a lost pet. The best reward for Glory is reuniting a missing animal and its human.

Molly, Coco, and a special friend

MOLLY and COCO: CONSERVATION CHAMPS!

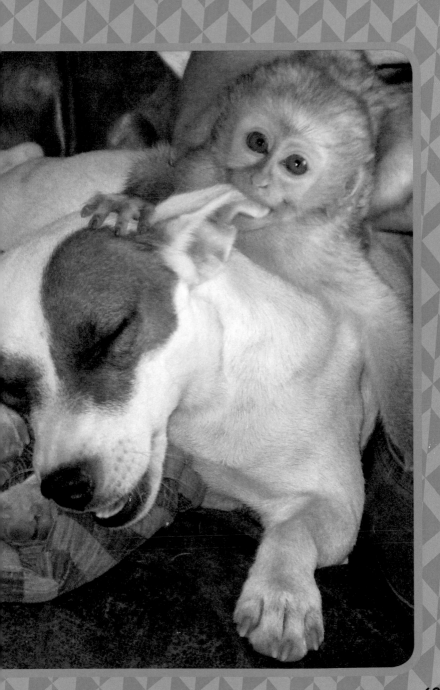

Molly and Coco greet their new friend.

Chapter 1

WELCOME HOME!

Molly and Coco trotted beside Anna Tolan in the big house in Africa. A new animal had arrived, and they wanted to meet him. The Jack Russell terriers loved welcoming wild animals to their home, the Chipembele (sounds like CHIP-em-beh-leh) Wildlife Education Trust, in Mfuwe, Zambia (sounds like Mm-FOO-ee, ZAM-bee-uh).

Molly and Coco greeted everyone who came, from small squirrels to large elephants. Anna and her husband, Steve, opened the door. Molly and Coco dashed outside. They raced over the dirt to a big covered pen called a boma (sounds like BO-mah). Something was moving inside!

Anna opened the gate. And there stood a baby hippopotamus! The dogs raced straight for the calf, then they jumped on him. *Lick, lick, lick.* They licked and licked his gray skin.

Douglas, the hippo, stayed very still. He didn't try to run. He didn't chase the dogs. Those licks felt good!

Molly and Coco continued to lick. *Welcome to Chipembele,* they seemed to say. *You are safe here, Douglas. We are friendly.*

Licking is how the dogs greet most newcomers, said Anna. That's how they say hello. The licking often calms the frightened animals, too. Most of the animals that come to Chipembele are motherless. Some are hurt. They are brought to the wildlife sanctuary (sounds like SANK-choo-air-ee) for care and medical treatment. The licking helps to relax them. If an animal is calm, it often eats better and heals more quickly.

There was a lot of Douglas to lick! This big baby weighed 111 pounds (50 kg). His size didn't stop the dogs, though. They licked Douglas all over, even his eyeballs! The little hippo was an orphan. Three months earlier, Douglas had been found alone in another part of Africa. He had been cared for by kind humans, but now he needed a bigger place, like Chipembele. The only problem: Chipembele was far away. To get to the sanctuary, Douglas and several caretakers had flown that morning in a plane, and then they had ridden in a truck. It had been a long day, and Douglas was tired. Douglas looked around the boma. Everything was strange! But Anna spoke to him calmly. So did Steve. They were the owners of Chipembele, and they made sure all the animals were safe and cared for. Molly and Coco gave Douglas a few more licks. The hippo relaxed. He drank some milk and went to sleep.

But soon he was awake again and hungry! Hippo calves eat a lot. For the next several days, three keepers cared for Douglas constantly. They fed him every three hours, day and night. Anna, Molly, and Coco checked on him often.

The dogs loved to visit their new friend. They especially liked what happened after he drank his milk. Douglas would open his huge mouth. The two dogs would put their heads inside. Douglas would hold very still. Then the dogs would lick up any last drops of milk. Molly and Coco had a little snack, thanks to Douglas.

The Power of Touch

Babies need more than food to survive. Many animal babies need to be held, touched, and groomed. This helps their brains and bodies to develop. Scientists have learned this by studying monkeys and rats. Animal babies that were not touched grew more slowly. They were nervous and depressed. When they became mothers, they did not care for their own babies very well. Touch continues to be important as children and animals grow into adulthood. It helps to lessen stress and worry. Have you ever gotten a hug from a friend when you were having a bad day or when you were sad? Did you feel better? That's the power of touch!

Douglas loved the attention and licks from the dogs. Their tongues probably felt a little like his mother's tongue. To grow big and healthy, many young animals need more than food. They also need to be stroked and groomed. They need to be cleaned and cuddled. In the wild, they usually receive this care from their mothers. But orphans like Douglas might get it from other animals or humans.

Some heroes do big, brave acts. Some, like Molly and Coco, are heroes by doing what they do every day at Chipembele. They help to care for baby animals that could not survive on their own. Over the years, the dogs have assisted with elephants, monkeys, warthogs, antelopes, and scrub hares. Douglas was their first baby hippo.

And they were doing a great job! So were Anna, Steve, and the other caretakers. Douglas grew bigger. After three days, it was time to show him the pond at Chipembele.

Anna and Steve knew that Douglas would love the pond. Wild hippos spend about 18 hours a day in the water. It helps to cool them and protect them from the hot African sun.

When he reached the pond, Douglas waded right in. The brown water slid over his skin. Ah, that felt good!

Soon it was time to return to his boma, but Douglas refused. He wanted to stay at the pond. *This is my new home,* he seemed to say. His caretakers agreed that this was best, too. At the pond, Douglas would learn how to take care of himself. Over time, like a wild hippo, he would begin to graze on the nearby grass. Douglas would learn to be independent.

But that didn't mean he was saying goodbye. The caretakers would need to bring milk to the pond until Douglas was one year old and could live completely on grass. Luckily, the pond wasn't far from the house. Anna, Steve, and the dogs could visit often. Douglas could also walk up to the yard. He still wanted his daily licks from Molly and Coco!

Molly and Coco keep their eyes on the road.

Chapter 2

Molly and Coco love to be busy. Jack Russell terriers are friendly and fearless. They like to go, go, go!

Whenever Anna or Steve open the door, the dogs race outside. They run to the wildlife sanctuary and to the bomas. *Time to visit,* they seem to say. Molly nuzzles a small antelope called a bushbuck. Coco sniffs an orphaned elephant.

The dogs greet the keepers who care for the animals. And who's that, coming around the corner? Douglas! The hippo lowers his head for some licks, and his buddies get busy. They lick his face, his ears, and of course, his eyeballs.

Sometimes Anna and Steve take the dogs to the pond. It is fun to watch Douglas play with his big plastic barrel. He likes to flop on top of it or push it through the water. The dogs want to swim with their friend, but this is dangerous.

A crocodile named Fluffy lives in the pond. Fluffy is a scaly reptile with a fierce bite. He doesn't bother Douglas. The hippo can protect himself with his powerful jaws. He can fight and maybe even kill a crocodile. But Fluffy would love to snack on a Jack Russell terrier. He cruises to the edge of the pond. Don't get too close, Molly and Coco!

Once they finish their outdoor visits, the dogs head for the house. They have already licked and comforted many animals, but they don't want to rest. No way! Jack Russell terriers love to work. Molly and Coco are ready for their next job: playing with baby monkeys!

They have been doing this job since they were puppies. "The baby monkeys would climb all over them," said Anna. They even pulled the dogs' ears. Ouch! But Molly and Coco never growled or snapped. They were always gentle with the babies.

A Dog Named Trump

Jack Russell terriers are named for
Reverend John (Jack) Russell, a pastor in
England. In the early 1800s, Jack bought
a female dog named Trump from a
milkman. She was fast, smart, small,
and lively. Trump was probably a mix of
different types of terrier, including the fox
terrier. Jack liked to hunt foxes, and
Trump was a big help. If a fox hid
underground, Trump squeezed into the

hole after it. She would dig for it with her strong paws. Trump didn't kill the fox, she only chased, or flushed, it out. Trump and her puppies were the first Jack Russell terriers. Today, many Jack Russell terriers are pets. They still have lots of energy and love to dig.

Although most of the wild animals stay outdoors, the baby monkeys live in the house. They sleep with Anna, Steve, Molly, and Coco, all in one big bed. Like baby humans, young monkeys need a lot of holding and cuddling. And like humans, it takes them a long time to grow up. During this time, they need to be carried and cared for. In this way, they learn to be healthy adults who can live and play with other monkeys. They also learn how to take care of their own babies.

At Chipembele, Mica (sounds like MI-ka) is the youngest monkey. He was only two weeks old when his mother was killed. At first, he had to be fed every two hours, so Anna kept him close to her. Mica is older now, but Anna still holds him often. He even sucks on her ear at night! Mica also likes to snuggle with Molly and Coco. And he does something that monkeys do with their mothers: He rides on their backs! He nibbles the food in their bowl, too. Yum!

Sometimes Mica joins Molly when she cuddles a lonely squirrel. Or when she curls up with a big-eyed bush baby. *The more the merrier,* Molly seems to say. The more warm bodies, the cozier everyone feels.

Mica is like all the creatures befriended by Molly and Coco. "The baby animals are very calm and relaxed in their presence," said Anna. "I've never seen any fear."

Molly tends to be calmer than Coco, and she likes to help Anna in another way. Teaching is the biggest job at Chipembele. Anna runs a program that teaches children about the plants and animals of Africa. The children go to school in their villages, but they take extra classes at Chipembele.

Before class starts, Molly sits in her favorite spot, under the teacher's table. She listens to the kids. They are so excited! They love learning about elephants, lions, and giraffes. Anna teaches them about conservation (sounds like kon-ser-VEY-shuhn), too. Conservation is the protection of wildlife. The children learn that wild animals need space to hunt and roam. They learn about poachers (sounds like POH-chers) who break the law by killing animals that are protected.

Conservation is serious stuff, but Anna's classes are fun! The kids draw pictures and play games. When they go home, they share their knowledge with friends and family. The students become teachers. They tell others how to protect animals.

Under the teacher's table, Molly suddenly sits up straight. Someone is poking his big gray head into the classroom. Douglas! *Hey, Molly,* he seems to say. *What's going on?* The children laugh.

Anna chases Douglas out, then a brown furry creature sneaks through an open window. A monkey! And he's stealing a pen! The children laugh again. Molly barks. Wildlife classes are always an adventure!

Anna and Steve have their hands full!

Chapter 3

PLAYTIME

Molly and Coco help wild animals in many ways. They are conservation champs! But once, Coco was the one who needed help.

The little dog was sitting in the end of Anna and Steve's boat. She loved to feel the wind in her furry face! Then—*bump!*—the boat hit a sandbar. Out flew Coco, right into the water. *Splash!*

The little dog surfaced, trying to swim. Molly barked. Anna and her two friends shouted. Steve didn't say anything. He dove into the river and rescued Coco. Everyone cheered.

Steve rescues wild animals, too. He is a volunteer wildlife police officer. He works hard to stop poachers. He searches for snares and traps. He searches for hunting camps. He looks for people who are cutting trees in protected areas. Cutting trees there is against the law. It destroys the homes, or habitats, of wild animals.

Molly and Coco always want to go with Steve. They run to the door. *Let us help,* they seem to say. But Steve has to be very quiet when looking for poachers. The dogs might bark and give him away.

Poachers might spot the dogs' white fur in the yellow grass. So Molly and Coco stay home with Anna. But they give Steve lots of welcome-home licks when he returns!

The dogs work hard, and they play hard, too. Their favorite game is catch. Steve throws the ball far, far into the bush. "They both tear after it with lightning speed," said Anna. The first one that finds the ball, brings it back. The dogs never tire of this game. "They will bark until Steve throws it again," said Anna.

Because Molly and Coco are so busy and fearless, Anna and Steve must watch them carefully. They like to chase the birds beside the pond. Storks, geese, and kingfishers flap into the air! If Fluffy is resting in the sun, the dogs try to nip him. It's not a good idea to tease a crocodile!

There are other dangers, too. At different times, both dogs have met a venomous snake called a cobra. Luckily, it didn't bite. But it did spray venom in their eyes. Thankfully, Anna and Steve were around. They quickly washed the dogs' eyes. That kept the terriers from going blind. Making sure that those lively dogs stay safe keeps Anna and Steve busy!

After a full day, Molly and Coco watch the sunset with their favorite humans. They eat dinner and play with the bush baby. They roll a tennis ball with the squirrel. Molly gives Mica a ride to bed. The two Jack Russell terriers stretch out. Time to sleep!

When morning arrives, the dogs bounce out of bed. They are eager for the day to begin! They like to oversee any changes at Chipembele. For example, Anna recently expanded the education program and hired four new teachers. Guess who helped to show these teachers around? Molly and Coco, of course! These teachers will be doing important work. They will travel to 17 village schools. They will help many more people to learn about conservation and how to protect wild animals.

The dogs oversee other changes as well. One big one: saying goodbye to the wild animals that have healed or grown old enough to care for themselves. This means it is time for them to return to the wild.

Remembering Rhinos

In Zambia, "chipembele" means "rhinoceros" in the local African language. At one time, black rhinos roamed freely in this part of Africa. Then poachers killed them in great numbers. They sold the horns for a lot of money. People used the horns for knife handles or fake medicines. Today the black rhino no longer exists in Zambia. Steve and Anna Tolan named their education center after the rhino. Classes at Chipembele Wildlife Education Trust focus on African plants and animals. The children learn how to conserve, or protect, wild things so they don't disappear from Zambia, like the black rhino did.

At Chipembele, any injured animals receive excellent care. Their wounds are cared for. They are given medicine if they are sick. Orphans like Douglas are first fed milk. Then they learn to find food.

"We like seeing the wild animals grow," said Anna. "We like seeing their wounds heal." She, Steve, and the dogs love getting to know each new creature. Each has a unique personality, from the cuddly little bush baby to big, playful Douglas.

The four miss the animals after they return to the wild. They have said goodbye to an elephant named Tafika and bushbucks named Sprite and Wanda. Anna and Steve feel sad, but they feel happy, too. "It is very rewarding," said Anna. "You know the animals are free to live in the wild again, where they belong."

Douglas may be at Chipembele for a few more years. He likes his pond. He does not want to join the wild hippos in the nearby river. Not yet, anyway. First, Douglas must grow bigger and stronger. Then he can protect himself from lions when he grazes. He can fight if male hippos attack him.

For Molly and Coco, that means more time with their big friend. They still get excited when they see him. *Lick, lick, lick.* Those conservation champs give Douglas the grooming he loves. Nose, cheeks, and eyeballs, too.

THE END

DON'T MISS!

NATIONAL GEOGRAPHIC KiDS **CHAPTERS**

LIVING WITH WOLVES!

True Stories of Adventures With Animals

Jim and Jamie Dutcher

Turn the page for a sneak preview . . .

KAMOTS: HOWLING WITH WOLVES!

These wolves join together for a group howl.

As a puppy, Kamots was very curious. Here he nibbles on a log to see what it tastes like.

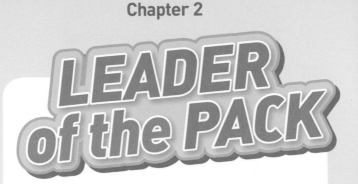

Chapter 2

LEADER of the PACK

Kamots wanted to explore everything. He and the other pups blew through the tent like little hurricanes. They snatched clothes, straps, tools, shoes—anything that wasn't nailed down. In minutes, they had chewed them to bits!

It was time for them to move out of the tent. But they were still too small for the big territory.

"What should we do with them?"
I asked my crew. "They need a safe place."
Then I figured it out. We fenced in an area
just outside the yurt. That way we could
keep an eye on them. And there would be
fewer things for them to chew on. Of
course, there was always the bottom of my
shirt to nibble. And
sometimes … *Ouch!*
That was my finger!

Within a few
months, I knew they
were ready for the big
enclosure. I felt like
I was sending my kids
off to school for the first time. I fumbled
with the latch while the pups jumped up
and whined with excitement. I opened the

gate, and they charged out. Guess who was right out in front? Kamots.

Kamots was fearless. He hopped onto a log and walked along it, like a tight-rope walker. When he was tired of that game, he wanted down. Jumping off was scarier than hopping on. But he only hesitated for a second. I could see that he had the gift of confidence.

The other pups followed Kamots around like he was in charge. I wasn't really surprised. I had noticed that Kamots was braver and more curious right from the start—a natural leader.

Every wolf pack needs a leader. The lead wolf is called the alpha (sounds like AL-fuh). He's like the captain of a ship. He goes first when they explore. If he senses danger, he makes sure the other wolves are safe before taking care of himself.

Before long, I saw other signs that Kamots was the alpha wolf. He howled first, keeping his head higher than the others when he did. *Arroooo!* And he was the first to greet human visitors. But the most astonishing sign came as soon as I began feeding the wolves like they were in the wild.

I fed them raw meat every three to five days. I talked to local officials. They allowed me to find dead animals that had been hit by cars. That way they wouldn't go to waste, and the wolves would have food to eat. Kamots ran to the food first.

But when the other wolves tried to join him, he glared at them and bared his teeth.

He snarled and flattened his ears. Even his brother, Lakota, had to wait his turn. I was shocked to see Kamots act like this. But then I understood. The alpha says who eats when. By telling the other wolves to wait, Kamots was telling them that he was in charge.

When Kamots growled at the others, he was acting like a parent scolding a child. There arc a lot of ways a wolf pack is like a family. I once heard about a wolf that was kicked in the jaw by a moose. His jaw was broken, and he couldn't chew meat. His pack chewed up food and fed it to him. Like a human family, they took care of a hurt member.

Arroooo!

Wolves howl for a lot of reasons. It doesn't seem to matter if the moon is out or not. Why do they howl? Sometimes it's to call to each other. Sometimes it's because they have a full belly. Often they howl because they enjoy it—it's like singing for them. Each wolf has a unique sound. We learned to identify which wolf was howling. We thought that Lakota had the prettiest howl. Wolves start howling when they are pups. But it sounds more like yodeling!

Only once did I ever see Kamots outsmarted. It was at dinnertime. And it took two wolves to do it. One wolf crept up, snatched a very small piece of meat and scampered off. His partner in crime waited his turn. As soon as Kamots ran after the first wolf with the meat, the second wolf lunged and grabbed a bigger chunk of meat. The second wolf raced off in the opposite direction. Kamots saw him out of the corner of his eye and chased him. Meanwhile, the first wolf ran back to dinner and grabbed an even larger hunk. Kamots never fell for this trick again!

Every morning, the wolves greeted each other . . .

INDEX

Boldface indicates illustrations.

MORE INFORMATION

To find out more information about the animals mentioned in this book, check out the links below.

Wilshire:
wilshirethefiredog.org

Chipembele Wildlife Education Trust:
chipembele.org

Lost Pet Detection:
lostpetdetection.com

CREDITS

To Harper and Lily, two heroic, amazing girls!
—MQ

ACKNOWLEDGMENTS

Many thanks to the following people who helped with this project:

Shelby Alinsky and Brenna Maloney, my amazing editors, and the entire National Geographic Kids Books staff.

Ryan Penrod of the Los Angeles Fire Department for generously sharing Wilshire's story, and to Ryan and his fellow firefighters for their service to the public.

Landa Coldiron of Lost Pet Detection for her kind assistance with Glory's tale.

Anna Tolan of the Chipembele Wildlife Education Trust, in Mfuwe, Zambia, for sharing vital details of Molly and Coco's adventures in Africa.

My large, loving family and many amazing friends in the children's book community. You are my heroes! And Yoshi, my furry muse.